The 2nd Bucks Battalion
OXFORDSHIRE AND BUCKINGHAMSHIRE LIGHT INFANTRY
1914–1918

Narrative compiled by
MAJOR - GENERAL
J. C. SWANN, C.B., D.L., J.P.
Secretary, Buckinghamshire
Territorial Force Association

The Naval & Military Press Ltd

Published by
The Naval & Military Press Ltd
5 Riverside, Brambleside, Bellbrook
Industrial Estate, Uckfield, East Sussex,
TN22 1QQ England

Tel: +44 (0) 1825 749494
Fax: +44 (0) 1825 765701

www.naval-military-press.com
www.nmarchive.com

In reprinting in facsimile from the original, any imperfections are inevitably reproduced and the quality may fall short of modern type and cartographic standards.

THE SECOND BUCKS BATTALION

THE Bucks Reserve Battalion, afterwards designated 2/1 Bucks Battalion (and commonly known as the 2nd Bucks), was raised at Aylesbury by Lt.-Col. H. M. Williams, T.D., and received official recognition on the 26th September, 1914. Lt.-Col. Williams at once began to look out for an officer of the Regular Army, if possible resident in the County, for the appointment of adjutant, and was able to obtain the services of Captain R. W. Harling, late The Connaught Rangers, residing at Little Hampden, who was gazetted on the 11th November. In the meantime the duties were carried on by Captain G. Christie-Miller, who had rejoined the 1st Battalion on mobilization from the T.F. Reserve, and had been transferred to the 2nd Battalion as one of the company commanders.

The other three companies were commanded by Captains H. L. C. Barrett, J. G. Hubbard (afterwards Lord Addington) and G. T. Hankin. Major J. H. Hooker was transferred from the 1st Battalion as 2nd in command, and held the appointment till May, 1915, when he was placed in command of the depot, and was succeeded by Major J. Chadwick as 2nd in command. Headquarters were established in Temple Square, the men being billeted in the town. The officers' Mess was located at the Bull's Head Hotel.

By the kindness of the O.C. Eton College O.T.C., Lt.-Col. Williams was able to obtain the loan of two excellent N.C.O. Instructors, Col.-Sergt. Dawes, of the Grenadier Guards, and Col.-Sergt. Carey, of the Rifle Brigade, for the training of recruits, in addition to several regular and ex-Regular N.C.O.'s of the Oxf. & Bucks. Lt. Infty. From the first, therefore, it was possible to set that high standard of discipline which was maintained by the Battalion throughout its service.

Recruiting proceeded rapidly, and the men were nearly all from the County, and a very good stamp. Leave was granted to N.C.O.'s and men to visit their homes and bring back recruits, and this was found to have very good results. In December the Band of the 1st Battalion joined, under Sergeant Brooks, from Wolverton, and proved a great asset to the Corps.

By the end of December the clothing and equipment of the Battalion was completed, and, as a considerable number of D.P. Rifles had been obtained on loan from the Eton O.T.C., the turn-out both on parade and in the streets of Aylesbury compared very favourably with the appearance of the battalions of Kitchener's Army in the vicinity, still in plain clothes or blue service uniforms and drilling with dummy rifles.

Lt.-Col. Williams showed great discrimination in his selection of officers to complete the establishment, from the large number of applicants for commissions in the Battalion, and from the first there existed a spirit of camaraderie and good fellowship amongst the officers which was reflected in the esprit de corps and the excellent feeling that grew up amongst all ranks and became so marked a feature throughout the corps, contributing in no small measure to that reputation for smartness and discipline which was borne by the Battalion in the 61st Division.

The first Christmas Dinner was held at the George Hotel and other centres, and shortly afterwards it became evident that the time for a move was getting near. Twice during January was the Battalion inspected, first by Lieut. General Sir R. Pole Carew, and later by Brigadier General the Marquis of Salisbury, and on both occasions their turn-out and their steadiness on parade were commended.

On the 1st February, the 2nd Bucks moved to Northampton and joined the South Midland Reserve Brigade, afterwards called the 184th Infantry Brigade, under command of Colonel Walter Ludlow, C.B., the other Battalions being the 2/4th R. Berks Regiment, the 2/4th Oxf. & Bucks. Lt. Infty. and the 2/5th Gloucester Regiment. This Brigade with the Warwick Infantry Brigade, afterwards the 182nd, and the Gloucester and Worcester Infantry Brigade, afterwards the 183rd, formed the Infantry of the 2nd South Midland Division, afterwards the 61st Division, under the command of Brigadier

General the Marquis of Salisbury, K.G., G.C.V.O.

Here the Battalion was armed with Japanese rifles, with 100 S.M.L.E. rifles for training purposes, and was provided with transport animals, horses and mules, many of them recent arrivals from the Argentine, U.S.A. and Canada. The transport drivers had little, if any, previous knowledge of horses, and had certainly never handled raw unbroken animals. They, however, tackled the job with energy, and, learning by experience, often painful, soon succeeded in getting the Battalion transport into working order, and eventually attained a high standard of turn-out and efficiency.

Battalion Headquarters were in Billing Road, the Officers' Mess in the cricket pavilion of the Asylum, and the cricket field was used as the parade ground. The Brigade training area comprised Great and Little Billing and Overstone Park. Platoon training was carried on and a musketry course fired with Japanese rifles, movements in Brigade were confined to route marching, occasionally by night.

The 61st Division was inspected in March at Northampton by General Sir Ian Hamilton, then G.O.C. in C. the Central Force. The weather was bad and the troops had to remain in line of massed battalions for a long time. This was the first appearance of the Battalion on a ceremonial parade of a large formation, and it emerged from the test with credit.

Early in April, 1915, the Division moved to Chelmsford where it formed part of the Third Army under General Sir Alfred Codrington, and took an active part in Home Defence.

The Battalion took over the billets in Springfield, which had been occupied by the first Battalion, before leaving for France. The parade ground and alarm post were in Queen's Park. Officers and men, who for various reasons were unfit for foreign service, were transferred to the 83rd Provisional Battalion then in course of formation under Lt.-Col. Martineau of the Warwicks in the Latchington Peninsula. Many of these men afterwards were drafted into the 10th Oxf. & Bucks. Lt. Infty. which formed part of the 215th Infantry Brigade in the 72nd Division at Ipswich.

Towards the end of April the 184th Brigade was detailed to work on the London Defences, and was allotted to the section Montnessing-Billericay, Brigade Headquarters being located at Epping. The Battalion was employed in digging trenches and their work, especially that under the direction of Major J. Chadwick, was specially commended. About three weeks were spent in this occupation, broken only by a sudden call to picket all the roads in the direction of London between Mountnessing, Billericay, Pitsford and the Coast near Southend, at an hour's notice. As the Battalion was far from complete in the matter of transport, a good deal of improvisation was necessary to get together the necessary carts, cars, etc., scattered detachments were called in, parties sent forward to arrange billets and locate bivouacs for the various posts. Material for barricades at cross roads was commandeered locally. The object of this emergency measure, which was extended all round the Metropolis, was the arrest of certain suspected persons and the examination of all motor cars and passers-by. These measures were continued for 48 hours, and afforded an excellent opportunity for officers and N.C.O.'s to cultivate initiative in fending for themselves and looking after the comfort of their men. Incidentally, whilst the Battalion was moving into position, the first Zeppelin air raid on Maldon took place. Shortly afterwards the Battalion returned to Chelmsford where they were again put through a musketry course, and Lewis Gun Training under Lt. Chadwick and Signalling under Lt. Wells were commenced. Large working parties for Ordnance Stores and Range Repairs had to be found in addition to the guard duties made heavier by the provision of anti-aircraft picquets and Aerodrome guards. The number of men available for training was thus much reduced and progress retarded.

It was, therefore, a welcome change when in June, 1915, the Brigade moved to Epping for a camp of instruction for six weeks.

Here training was carried out by platoons and companies on the excellent terrain comprised in Epping Forest, and officers were exercised in independent command of their platoons and companies making their own schemes and arrangements for bivouacs, rations, etc. Whilst thus engaged the Lord Lieutenant (The Marquess of Lincolnshire), and several members of the Territorial Force Association, visited the camp and were greatly interested in the progress that had been made by the Battalion. Returning to Chelmsford Battalion and Brigade training was continued through the summer and autumn. Entrenching ground was secured for the Brigade near Boreham, and on the Chelmsford-Chignall Smealy Road, trenches were dug and occupied, and battalions exercised in trench warfare, though timber, wire, lights, flares and other paraphernalia were not as yet available for training purposes. At this time the elaborate system of bombing and trench warfare grounds established at home at command, army and T.R. Centre Schools was not yet in existence. The only bombing school available for the Brigade was at Witham with a more advanced school for selected officers in Sussex, under the control of the Central Force. Bombing and rifle grenade training were in fact in their infancy. Training in these subjects in a battalion, therefore, depended in a greater degree on the individual initiative of officers than was the case in the later stages of the war.

It is, however, quite open to argument whether the officers and men, for the most part raw troops, did not gain more in initiative and discipline from the training they received at this time in open warfare, march discipline, use of ground, etc., than would have been the case had their training been limited by the necessity of undergoing a more exacting course of trench warfare.

In July, the Division was inspected by Sir Leslie Rundle, G.O.C. in C., Central Force, and on the 6th August by Field Marshal Earl Kitchener at Hylands Park. After the general salute had been given in line of close columns, the Brigades marched past in column of fours, each battalion headed by its band.

It was generally believed at the time, and as events proved not without reason, that the employment of 2nd line formations as such with the B.E.F. was finally decided upon by the authorities as the result of this inspection. Whether this was a fact or not, it is certain that the physique, turn-out, *esprit de corps*, and the general progress that had been made by corps towards efficiency made a very favourable impression on the mind of Lord Kitchener, and this may have been an important factor in the decision, when the matter of the disposal of the 2nd line formations came up for decision.

In September, in order to meet the pressing demands for drafts to replace casualties in France, the establishment of all second line infantry units was reduced to 22 officers and 600 O.R., the surplus being drafted overseas, or, if unfit, sent to third line units.

In November, Brig.-General Lord Salisbury relinquished the command of the 61st Division and was succeeded by Major General Bannatine Allason, who, however, was soon transferred to command a Division at Perth, and Major General Colin Mackenzie was appointed to the command of the 61st Division shortly before they moved to Salisbury Plain in February.

Here the Battalion was quartered in huts at Parkhouse Camp. Intensive training was carried out in preparation for overseas, and units were brought up to war strength again by drafts mostly found by Provisional Battalions, and composed chiefly of men from the Liverpool, Herts, Suffolk and Cambridge Regiments.

In April, the Division had the honour of being inspected by H.M. King George, in anticipation of their departure to join the B.E.F. in the following month. On this occasion the Battalion showed up well, and elicited favourable comment.

Major Chadwick left the Battalion about this time to join the 2nd Garrison Battalion Oxf. & Bucks. Lt. Infty. with which he proceeded to France, afterwards commanding a Labour Battalion.

Captain G. Christie-Miller was promoted Major and succeeded him as 2nd in Command, and Captain G. E. W. Bowyer became Adjutant vice Major Christie-Miller.

On 25th May, 1916, the Battalion left Parkhouse Camp and entrained for Southampton where it embarked for Havre.

Before leaving for France distinctive symbols were allotted to all units of the Division, and a Divisional mark adopted formed of the number of the Division in Roman numerals which were allowed to touch (LXI). The Brigades were distinguished by the shape, the units by the colour of the patches an inch in diameter worn on the upper sleeve of both arms. The 182nd Brigade had squares, the 183rd triangles, the 184th circles, and in the Brigades the

Senior Battalion wore scarlet, 2nd Senior bright blue, 3rd Senior yellow, and the Junior black, machine gun companies apple green, and L.T.M. Batteries purple or brown. These marks were painted on all vehicles, together with the Divisional symbol, and on sign boards for Headquarters. They were also generally placed on the steel helmets of the men.

On arrival at Havre the Battalion entrained for the front, Divisional Headquarters being at St. Venant, and Brigade Headquarters at Les Lauriers on the border of the Foret de Nieppe. They detrained at Berguette and marched to billets at Le Sart near Merville. Here they remained for about ten days before they and the 2/4th R. Berks were ordered up to Laventie to take the place of the 2/5th Gloucesters and 2/4 Oxfords, who were undergoing their training in the trenches attached to units of the 114th Brigade of the 38th Welsh Division. Two days later the 184th Brigade was sent to relieve the 114th in the Fauquissart Section, and the Bucks and Berks Battalions took over the line with the Oxfords and Gloucesters in reserve. This was a curious take over. It involved a walk down the front line from the Ducks Bill. It was carried out in daylight and without previous reconnaisance. Battalion Headquarters were established at the White House on Bacquerot Street (the right sub-section of the Fauquissart Section).

The tours of duty in the trenches were arranged at first so that Battalions had four days in the line and four in reserve. These tours were lengthened later. The Oxfords relieved and were relieved by the R. Berks, the Gloucesters by the Bucks, the former Battalions taking the left, the latter the right sub-section.

On July 3rd, the Battalion was withdrawn to rest billets at La Fosse, but on arrival at that place was ordered almost immediately to march to take over the right sub-section of the Ferme de Bois section from a Battalion of the 91st Infantry Brigade.

Battalion Headquarters were established in a building near Windy Corner on the road leading from Richebourg St· Vaast-Richebourg L'Avoue. Whilst in reserve, Battalion Headquarters were in a house opposite the Church at R.

St. Vaast, situated on the St. Vaast-Croix Barbee Road.

After some two weeks in this sub-section the Battalion was withdrawn on 15th July and marched back to Laventie, where preparations were begun for the attack which eventually took place on the 19th July, 1916, after being postponed from the 17th.

The object in view by the Division was to render assistance to the operations on the Somme by preventing the withdrawal of German troops from this sector as reinforcements.

The Division was closed up on less than a brigade frontage from opposite the Wick to Sugar Loaf salients, two battalions from each Brigade were detailed for this attack, the remaining two being in support.

Of the 184th Brigade the R. Berks were detailed for the right, the Bucks for the left of the attack. The 183rd Brigade were on the right of the R. Berks, the Australians on the left of the Bucks, but owing to the salient unable to keep in touch.

Battalion Headquarters were at a farm in front of Picantin Post between that post and Jocks Lodge.

The Oxfords and Gloucesters were in support and reserve near Sailly and at Estaires, and moved up during the attack to positions in front of Bacquerot Street and to some strong posts in the vicinity.

The formation of dumps of S.A.A. rations, water, engineer stores, etc., necessitated heavy fatique work for days beforehand, and even the troops detailed for the attack were not exempt up to the last moment.

The preliminary bombardment which lasted for three days was carried out by some 350 guns of all calibres, R.F.A. and R.H.A. Batteries being pushed up to within a short distance of Tilleloy Street, many of them in exposed positions, where they suffered heavy casualties. On the afternoon of the 19th, " lifts to barrage lines " were ordered for the artillery for certain periods, varying from four to ten minutes during which the infantry in the trenches were to show their bayonets, and steel helmets, over the parapets, and officers were to whistle and shout orders with the view of inducing the enemy to man his parapet and thereby incur heavy casualties, when the artillery shortened the range on to the front parapet and continued the intense bombardment of the front and support lines.

During the last phase of the bombardment the attacking infantry was to issue through the sally ports and gaps cut in their wire and deploy in No Man's Land in four waves, the leading wave within 80 yards of the enemy's parapet, if possible, and 50 yards between waves. The assault was timed for 6 p.m.

In the Battalion A Company, commanded by Captain H. Church, and D, commanded by Captain I. Stewart-Liberty, were detailed for the attack. On the 18th, A Company had lost 78 men owing to a short shell from one of our own guns falling on a gas cylinder and bursting it in the trench. This had necessitated filling up the ranks of the Company with men from the reserve and from a newly-arrived draft, but it was still much under strength. On the 19th, owing to the restricted front and consequent crowding in the trenches, the casualties were very heavy amounting to nearly 100 killed and wounded before the companies moved out to deploy for the assault. Luckily, it was not necessary to use the sally ports, which in the case of other units caused heavy losses at the start, as they had been located by the enemy, and were effectively covered by machine gun fire. A better way had been found, and at 5-40 p.m. the assaulting companies filed out into No Man's Land by way of Rhondda Sap and lay down in four waves. In order to complete the waves C Company, commanded by H. S. G. Buckmaster, had followed A and D, and B, commanded by Captain R. F. Symonds, moved in to hold and garrison the line.

At 6 p.m., with a cheer the four waves leaped up and assaulted the enemy's trenches. The advance was described by an officer of the R.A.F., observing for the Artillery, as magnificent. Not a man was seen to waver, but the fire brought to bear was annihilating. Even before 5-40 p.m. the enemy machine guns had begun to get busy, and at 6 p.m. they literally mowed down the advancing waves; only a few men actually reached the German parapet, some were seen actually on the parapet, and may have got in, but none got back.

By 6-30 p.m. it was evident that the attack had failed,

but it has been asserted that success could have been secured had it been possible to bring two fresh companies to the assault. No reserves, however, were available; B Company was fairly intact, but definitely marked for garrison duty in the line—a few orderlies, telephone operators, etc., were with Headquarters, and the small remnant of the assaulting companies, who survived, were in No Man's Land awaiting darkness to get back. All the officers of the three companies that had gone out were either killed or wounded except one. The position was reported to the Brigade Headquarters and orders received to re-organize and attack again at 8-30 p.m. Re-organization was effected so far as possible by taking 40 men from B Company and collecting about 80 more from the other companies. As soon as this had been carried out, orders were received first, postponing, and finally cancelling the fresh attack.

In hardly any other portion of the attack of the two Divisions was any greater success obtained. A party of the Worcesters on the right, opposite Fauquissart, gained a footing in the enemy's line, but could not be supported, and few were able to get back. The same thing happened to an Australian Battalion on the left. On no other part of the line was any impression made. The attack, therefore, though successful in preventing the withdrawal of Infantry or guns to reinforce in withstanding the offensive on the Somme, failed to gain the local objective, "the capture and occupation of the German front and support line on this side of the river Layes."

Incidentally the enemy incurred heavy casualties though not nearly so heavy as was calculated during the progress of the bombardment. Their line was lightly held by infantry, great reliance being placed on their numerous and well-trained machine gun teams, their bomb-proof shelters were efficient, and they persistently declined to be misled by the appearances of imminent attack stage-managed for their benefit. Yet at the moment of the real attack they were all there; and from the action of their machine gun teams it would seem that their Intelligence officers had "inferred" zero with considerable accuracy.

The casualties in the Battalion, which had gone into

action with 20 officers and 622 other ranks, were 322 of all ranks during the 18th and 19th July.

KILLED.

Capt. H. Church. 2nd Lt. H. R. N. Brewin.
Lieut. C. P. Phipps. 2nd Lt. F. R. Parker.
       and 62 other ranks.

DIED OF WOUNDS.
Lieut. D. G. Chadwick.

WOUNDED.

Capt. I. Stewart-Liberty. 2nd Lt. B. H. Drakes.
Capt. V. W. G. Ranger. 2nd Lt. G. D. W. Oliver.
2nd Lt. H. G. Baddeley. 2nd Lt. T. J. Relf.
2nd Lt. A. T. Pitcher. 2nd Lt. J. S. Rutherford.
       and 180 other ranks.

MISSING (all believed killed).
Lieut. G. W. Atkinson. 2nd Lt. R. B. Hudson.
       and 65 other ranks.

For conspicuous services rendered during this action the Military Cross was awarded to Captain I. Stewart-Liberty, Capt. J. E. S. Wilson (R.A.M.C.), 2nd Lieut. B. H. Drakes, 2nd Lieut. A. H. Phillips; the Distinguished Conduct Medal to R.S.M. E. Jones and Corporal F. Gurney; and the Military Medal to Sergeant J. Petty, Corporal T. Oldroyd, Corporal S. R. Hayers, Lance-Corporal R. Francklowe, Private W. Sanders.

At 1 a.m. on the 20th, the Battalion, on relief by the 2/4th Oxfords, withdrew to its billets near Laventie, and at 10 a.m. was conveyed by motor bus to Estaires.

In a Division Order of that date the G.O.C. expressed his appreciation of the conduct of all arms on the previous days, " The Division has not only fought gallantly, but all ranks in every arm and service have carried out in the most exemplary and devoted manner, working day and night, an amount of work which has highly tested their endurance and discipline and merits my unqualified praise."

On the following date G.H.Q. wired to the Division, " Please convey to the troops engaged on night of 19th, 20th, my appreciation of the gallant effort and the thorough preparation made for it. I wish them to realize that their enterprise has not been by any means in vain, and the gallantry, with which they carried out the attack, is fully recognised.—Chief."

On the 22nd the Battalion was inspected by Major General Colin Mackenzie, Commanding the 61st Division. The strength of the Battalion on paper was 19 officers and 545 other ranks, but the muster on parade was very different. B was a fair sized Company, C was represented by two platoons of medium strength, but the rest of the Battalion produced a mere handful of men, and practically no N.C.O.'s. Major H. L. C. Barrett and Captain H. S. G. Buckmaster had just been invalided to England, the Battalion thus losing the last of its four Company Commanders. Except in B Company there were no company officers of any experience left, and the vacancies had been filled by recent postings, new and as yet untried.

The work of re-organization was started at once, and carried on as rapidly as possible. On the 24th, a move was made to Riez Bailleul, and on the 27th two companies went into the line in the Moated Grange sub-section, the other two companies occupying ten posts.

On the last day of the month, to the great regret of all ranks in the Battalion, Lt.-Col. H. M. Williams handed over the command to Major G. Christie-Miller, pending the arrival of Major J. B. Muir (4th Black Watch), who was appointed to succeed him, and joined on 5th August.

During the period of nearly two years in which he commanded the Battalion, Colonel Williams had won the respect and esteem of all under his command. His long connection with the Bucks Battalion had given him a thorough understanding of the citizen soldier, his business ability enabled him to deal successfully with the administrative side of his duties, whilst his close study of military subjects was shown by the high standard of efficiency attained by the Battalion in training and the way in which he handled it in action. During the whole of the seven hours' bombardment on the 19th, he was in the front line setting a fine example to his men of coolness under fire, and had personally superintended the re-organisation of the Battalion after the attack. His services were recognised later by mention in despatches, and he was appointed Town Commandant of Arras, and in the German retreat of 1918 became Area Commandant of Douai.

Brigadier General W. J. Dugan, D.S.O., took over command of the 184th Brigade at this time from Brigadier General C. H. P. Carter, but did not hold it for long, as he was accidently wounded in the middle of September whilst watching a trench mortar demonstration at Meurillon. He, however, made a successful recovery and was appointed later to the command of another Brigade, where doubtless he became as popular as he had been during his short stay with the 184th.

The Battalion moved into billets at Le Grand Pacaut, three drafts amounting to just over 100 men in all were received, though not sufficient to bring the strength up to the establishment.

On the 5th August, Major J. B. Muir arrived and took over the command of the Battalion from Major Christie-Miller, and was gazetted Lt.-Colonel.

The task that lay before him was not an easy one. The Battalion had been knocked to pieces, few officers and N.C.O.'s of any experience remained, drafts in every stage of efficiency and inefficiency were being sent to fill up, the material was good, but much had to be done before the 2nd Bucks regained its standard of efficiency. Lt.-Col. Muir had the experience of a dozen years' service with Territorials, in peace and war, firmness, tact and last but not least a keen sense of humour, in giving expression to which he was a past master. From the first his popularity was assured, and his hold on all ranks strengthened as time went on. His ready appreciation of all that was good was matched by his candid but kindly criticism of lapses from the standard of the corps. The old nucleus that remained was good, the new drafts quickly became imbued with the esprit de corps that was so marked a feature of the Battalion, all ranks were keen. Under these conditions progress was rapid during the weeks of comparative quiet in the line in the Moated Grange sector with periods of rest at Riez Bailleul.

On 8th September a bombing accident occurred, due to a premature explosion. The Battalion Quartermaster, Lieut.

D. Waller was wounded, losing his hand, the bombing officer, 2nd Lt. A. J. Smee, attached from 3rd Wilts, and 4 other ranks were wounded, and three men were killed.

On 30th September, Brigadier General The Hon. R. White, C.M.G., succeeded to the vacancy in the Brigade Command caused by the accident to Brigadier General Dugan. During this period and up to the 28th October, the Battalion continued to relieve and be relieved by the 2/5th Gloucesters every six days, going into billets at Riez Bailleul when out of the trenches, and were most efficiently covered by the same Battery (C.306) commanded by Captain Duncan.

On 29th October the Battalion marched to billets near Robecq where the next few days were spent in open warfare training. During the past two months owing to the amount of work on the defences, etc., imposed on corps it had been extremely difficult to arrange for the training so urgently required in view of the number of young officers and N.C.O.'s with the unit. Every opportunity, therefore, was welcomed, and several occurred on the march to the Somme, after leaving Robecq on 2nd November.

The route taken was by Auchelle–Monchy Breton–Averdoigt Rebreuviette–Barly–Montrelet–Harponville to Albert, which was reached on 19th November. Throughout this 90 mile march, though the weight carried by each man was between 70-80 lbs., and the distances covered were considerable, not a man of the Bucks Battalion fell out, a record of the march discipline that had been instilled into the men, and it may be added, a tribute to the personality of the Battalion Medical Officer, Captain J. E. S. Wilson, who seemed to possess the power of persuading a tired man that fatigue was an illusion, and of stimulating him to fresh exertion.

At Albert for the first time the two Bucks Battalions met, the 1/1st being in the line near the Butte de Warlencourt. During the subsequent operations on the Somme, only one Division lay between the 48th and 61st Divisions in the line.

On the 21st November, the 61st Division relieved the 18th, the 184th Brigade relieving the 55th, the Bucks Battalion being in Brigade Reserve at Ovillers where they remained till they moved up to the Mouquet Farm right sub-section in relief of the 2/5th Gloucesters on the 26th. On the 30th the Brigade went into Divisional Reserve, the Battalion moving to Martinsart Wood, and thence to Hedauville where they spent a week training.

On the 11th December, Captain and Adjutant G. E. W. Bowyer left to be attached to the staff of the Division, and 2nd Lieut. T. S. Markham was appointed to act as Adjutant in his place. On the 12th, the Battalion moved up to Martinsart, and were employed on many and various fatigues till the 20th, when they moved to Wellington Huts via Aveluy, in support, with A Company in Fabeck Trench, and on the 24th went into the line Desire Trench.

This trench, which had recently been captured from the enemy, lay at the bottom of the valley some 500 yards in advance of Regina and 2nd Assembly Trenches, and all were commanded from the German position at Grandcourt on the opposite rise, so that all movements by day were clearly visible. The trenches and approaches were deep in mud, and inter company reliefs were often delayed by the difficulty of finding the way, and the weather seemed to get worse and worse every day. Despite the wet and mud the Battalion managed to spend a cheery Christmas Day, and sent a Christmas greeting to the First Bucks.

On the 30th December the Brigade moved back into Reserve, the Battalion going to Hedauville, where they were able to do some strenuous training before they were again in support in Martinsart Wood on the 8th, and employed on working parties till the 14th.

On the 15th, the Battalion left for Gappennes in the Abbeville area for rest and training, marching via Puchvillers, Gezaincourt, in heavy snow, and Mesnil-Domqueur. At Gappennes they were accommodated in huts and barns and underwent training in very cold and frosty weather till the 3rd February, when orders were received to move to the neighbourhood of Ablaincourt. Marching by Villers, where a halt of 8 days allowed training to be continued, they entrained on the 13th at Longpre for Marcelcave and thence marched via Wiencourt Camp to Framerville, and on the 16th February relieved the 1st Battalion of the 124th French Regiment in Deniecourt northern sub-section. When first taken over, in a slight frost, the trenches seemed to compare more than favourably with anything that the Battalion had so far seen in that line. They were narrow and deep, well supplied with serviceable dug-outs, and beautifully duckboarded. But when the frost disappeared the total absence of revetting allowed the whole to collapse rapidly, and the rain that followed the thaw turned every trench into a holding morass of knee deep slime.

In this locality, varied by a week's training at Rainecourt, the Battalion remained till the withdrawal of the Germans became known and the 61st Division began to move forward on the 18th March. The Battalion was then at Vauvillers, resting and training and advanced via Lihons, Vermandovillers, Bersaucourt, Marchelepot and Flez and Douvieux, halting to repair roads and fill in mine craters as they proceeded. The villages were found in a most deplorable state, largely owing to deliberate damage, buildings burnt to the ground, trees cut down, wells contaminated with filth, etc. Nothing in fact in the way of destruction, that was possible, had been left undone.

On 30th March, the Battalion marched to Montecourt and thence to Tertry and on 1st April relieved the 2/8th Warwicks in the line at Soyecourt, a village two miles in front of Tertry, but reduced to ruins. Sufficient material, timber and corrugated iron was, however, found amongst the debris to enable the men to construct shelters for themselves. Warning of an attack to be made the following morning was received but too late for a thorough reconnaissance of the enemy's position. A reconnoitring patrol was, however, sent out at dusk under Lieut. Petrie to ascertain whether the Montolu Woods were occupied or the approaches to the railway embankment guarded. A small sentry group disappeared from the woods on the approach of the patrol, but no other Germans were discovered in the localities mentioned.

The enemy was holding a line through Bihecourt northwards along a ridge north-east of Soyecourt with the Bihecourt–Vendelles Road and the railway embankment in front of their position. The attack of the 184th Brigade was to be made by the Bucks and R. Berks. On their left was the 59th Division with the right Battalion of which, the

Sherwood Foresters, the 2nd Bucks had to keep in touch. On the right of the R. Berks came the 183rd Brigade. The attacking companies were to advance at 5 a.m. on 2nd April from the embankment, while the artillery shelled the enemy, and the 184th Machine Gun Company supported the advancing infantry with overhead fire. In the Battalion, C Company under Captain Beck, and D Company under Captain Tyler, were detailed for the attack, two platoons of A to cover the left flank, and B Company to hold the original line. Guided by a telephone line and keeping position by a second line of wire 900 yards long, which each man held in his left hand, the companies moved in file to a point on the embankment, and then turning right handed deployed along it, each Company having a frontage of 450 yards. The wire obtained for the guide line had evidently been classed as " unserviceable " as it parted at intervals, causing delays till joined up again. The deployment, however, was completed just in time. At 5 a.m. the guns opened fire, and the men advanced. D Company on the left met with no opposition and as they topped the ridge they saw the enemy completely taken by surprise making off in every direction. C Company on the right met with more opposition, and in addition suffered some casualties from our own barrage, either from shorts, or from pressing on too eagerly before it had lifted forward. Captain Beck was wounded in the hand, but continued to lead his men forward with great gallantry until he fell mortally wounded. Later this Company also came in for a burst of Lewis gun-fire from a part of another Battalion, which had attacked and captured Bihecourt, and issuing from that village mistook them in the grey light of dawn for Germans. Apart from these contretemps the attack was completely successful, several prisoners were taken and the captured positions were consolidated. The Battalion lost Captain Beck and 8 other ranks killed, Lieut. Hughes and 29 other ranks wounded.

The F.M. Commanding-in-Chief expressed his satisfaction at the recent operations of the Division, and the Battalion was thanked by the Brigadier for the share they had taken. Before the Battalion went out of the line they had made a further advance and occupied Caubrieres Wood, and on return to Soyecourt on 7th April, after three days at Coulincourt, were able to occupy the trenches on the ridge forming part of the new German position which had been attacked without success on the 6th by the Gloucesters and Oxfords. A patrol of B Company, under Lieut. Foster, on the night of the 8th, discovered that they had been evacuated, though a patrol of the Berkshires on the right had found them occupied only a short time before. On receipt of the information the Berkshires and the 59th Division on the left also moved up to the vacated positions.

On the 10th April, the Battalion was relieved in the line by the 18th H.L.I. of the 106th Brigade, 35th Division, and on the 12th marched to Offoy on the banks of the Somme, where a week was spent in training and cleaning before they moved to Germaine on the 19th, and on the next day went into support at Holnon, the left section of the Divisional front, one Battalion of the 184th Brigade holding an outpost line about 1,000 yards to the east of the village of Fayet This line, as well as Fayet itself and the main line of resistance 800 yards in front of Holnon, was all under the observation of the enemy at St. Quentin. The Battalion was employed nightly in digging and wiring the resistance line till they relieved the 2/5th Gloucesters in the out-post line, on the night of the 23rd–24th.

During the night of the 25th, the Battalion took over a fresh line of posts, thus extending the line about 1,000 yards to the South East. Just in front of the right flank, where a sharp salient existed in the line, lay Cepy Farm. This farm had been captured by the 32nd Division, who had, however, been shelled out of it later. A reconnaisance under Lieut. Pitcher found it unoccupied. At 7 p.m. on the next day a strong attack developed by a picked force of stormers. The amount of dead ground and the inherent weakness of the salient favoured an attack from the direction of Cepy Farm, from which a sunken road running north-west passed through the centre of the line of outposts, but had been closed by a barrier; an old German trench also provided an approach from the farm to the barrier. Making use of this trench and the sunken road one party of the enemy issuing from the farm made for the barrier whilst another party attempted to surround the adjacent post.

The attack on the post failed, excellent work being done by Corporal Hopcraft, with his Lewis gun, and Sergeant Clarke with two bombers, the former unfortunately being killed. A third party of the enemy attacked a post a little further north but were promptly met by Lewis gun fire, and as they retired were followed by Corporal Brawn with a party of bombers, who succeeded in killing five and capturing six prisoners. The attack was thus completely broken up, more than twenty of the enemy having been killed and few, if any, escaping unwounded. The casualties in the Battalion were one man killed and two wounded.

For their services on this occasion C.S.M. Hearn, Sergeant Clarke and Corporal Brawn received the D.C.M., and Corporal Windsor the Military Medal.

The same night the Battalion was relieved and bivouacked at Attilly, moving into support outside Holnon on the 29th, and resuming work on the resistance line.

After another tour in the outpost line the Battalion moved to Germaine, and spent the time in training, when not employed on working parties, till the 15th May, when they proceeded via Amiens to Arras, arriving on 31st, and moving into support at Marliere and Wancourt the next day, and into the line east of Guemappe on the 6th June.

On relief by the 2nd London Regiment the Battalion spent some ten days at Berneville training. Capt. R. F. Symonds was appointed Adjutant. Drafts began to arrive, and they had been badly wanted, as the strength of the companies had fallen to A 110, B 90, C 70, D 90. On the 23rd June, the Battalion entrained at Gouy for Auxi-le-Chateau and thence marched via Frohen le Grand to Rouge Fay where four weeks were spent in training before going into the Ypres area. Drafts continued to arrive but the larger number only joined when more than half the time allotted for training had passed. This not only increased the difficulties, but also tended to lower the whole standard during the more advanced training. Luckily further opportunity occurred on arrival in the Lederzele–Rubruick area on 26th July, and training was continued throughout the first half of August.

On the 15th August the Battalion moved to Abeele,

and on the 18th to Goldfish Chateau Camp near Ypres. On the evening of the 20th they advanced to the support line just forward of Wieltje, having many casualties on the way from shell fire. After dark they went into the line in the Pommern Castle Sector, Headquarters at Uhlan Farm, C Company on the left, B on the right (front line) D left support, A right support. The next day was spent in preparations for the attack on the 22nd.

Of the 61st Division the 184th Brigade was told off for the attack, having the 44th Infantry Brigade, 15th Division, on their right, and the 143rd Brigade, 48th Division, on their left. The Bucks were to make the attack on the right, the Oxfords on the left of the Brigade, each Battalion taking a frontage of approximately 700 yards.

The Bucks were to advance with two companies forming the first and second waves, and two companies forming the third and fourth; the Oxfords were to attack with three companies forming the first and second and one company the third wave. Eight platoons of the R. Berks were to be attached to the Bucks as "moppers up," and five to the Oxfords. The Gloucesters and one battalion of the 183rd Brigade were in Brigade Reserve.

The final objective was the position on the Kansas Cross–Winnipeg Road. The "moppers up" were to deal with the strong posts at Somme, Aisne, Gunpits, Cross Cotts, Green House, Martha, Kier Farm, and various dug-outs, and to be ready to cover the flanks if necessary. This would enable the main attack to push forward to take the main position without delaying to clear the strong points in advance of it.

At 4-45 a.m. the Artillery put down the barrage and the waves advanced, disregarding the strong posts and pressing forward as close as possible to the barrage in accordance with the orders they had received. The "moppers up," in attempting to follow, suffered heavily in casualties from machine gun and rifle fire; the garrisons of the posts, behind their concrete walls, put up a stubborn resistance. The Somme and Aisne Farms were taken, but the latter retaken almost at once by the enemy. Pond Farm in front of the Oxfords on the left and Gallipoli in fornt of the 7th Cameron Highlanders on the right remained in the possession of the enemy. The position of the advancing waves of the Bucks became more and more serious, but still they pressed on, and some at least reached their objective, though exposed to fire from front, flanks and rear, and entirely cut off from all communication. Meanwhile a company of the 2/5th Gloucesters under 2nd Lieut. Johnston, with the few remaining men available with the Battalion, consolidated a line of shell holes for the defence of Somme Farm that had been won by a platoon of the Berks, only three men of which remained to follow 2nd Lieut. St. Leger into the post and to deal with the 14 survivors of the garrison. Three counter attacks were made on the newly-consolidated line, but were caught by the fire of our artillery, and easily repulsed by the infantry. The enemy snipers were much in evidence throughout the day, any movement that might suggest a runner with information for Headquarters attracted their special attention; even stretcher bearers and wounded crawling painfully back were not spared.

At 4 p.m., with the assistance of two platoons of the 2/5th Gloucesters, the Oxfords finally assaulted and captured Pond Farm. This much relieved the pressure on the left of the Bucks, and they were able to straighten out the line. A party was sent forward to take the gunpits, but found them deserted by the enemy but giving shelter to many of the wounded of the Battalion, including 2nd Lieut. S. A. G. Gibson, who had shown conspicuous gallantry in the attack and was awarded the Military Cross before he died of his wounds.

The losses were found to have been very heavy; 13 company officers and 637 other ranks went into action, 11 officers and 338 other ranks were reported as casualties.

KILLED : 2nd Lieut. C R. Tyson and 46 other ranks.

DIED OF WOUNDS : Capt. J. E. S. Wilson, R.A.M.C., 2nd Lieut. Gibson, 2nd Lieut. W. R. Gill.

WOUNDED : Capt. G. C. Stevens, 2nd Lieut. T. S. Markham, 2nd Lieut. G. P. Steed, 2nd Lieut. W. H. Petrie, and 156 other ranks.

MISSING : Capt. H. R. Foster, 2nd Lieut. H. E. Molloy, 2nd Lieut. W. E. Rolfe, and 122 other ranks (presumed dead).

Of the missing, 19 were afterwards traced as prisoners of war, and 103 presumed killed. 9 of the prisoners were wounded when captured. At night the Battalion was relieved by the 2/7th Worcesters, to whom they handed over a much improved line, straighter and stronger than it had been when they took it over on the 20th. Many attempts were made by the Worcesters and Warwicks to clear the strong posts and gun pits in front during their tour in the line, but without achieving any success, and they remained an annoyance until swept away in the general attack and advance on the 1st October.

The Battalion returned to their old bivouac at Goldfish Chateau; a sad return. Except A Company, all were commanded by Sergeants. The men were in the last stage of exhaustion; the strongest Company had barely 80, the weakest just over 50 in the ranks.

Practically all the officers had become casualties at the very commencement of the action, despite the fact that in accordance with orders they wore the dress and equipment of the men. This shows that in fighting at short range it is the act of leadership rather than the dress that distinguishes the officer as a mark to be specially selected.

Captain Wilson was a great loss to the Battalion, to which he had been devoted. His ready sympathy, unfailing cheerfulness and keen insight into character gave him an influence with officers and men which he ever exerted in the interests of the corps, and the maintenance of esprit de corps, and a high sense of duty. A brilliant writer, no mean artist, and an able organizer, he took a leading part in arranging the social entertainments that brightened the strenuous days, when opportunity offered during periods of training behind the line.

After one night at Goldfish Chateau the Battalion moved back to Brandhoek. Here they found themselves in a camp that seemed luxurious in comparison with any of the quarters they had occupied in France. It was duck boarded throughout and very clean, the accommodation for the men was ample and good provision existed for the administrative offices. The officers' lines contained mess room and ante room on a large scale, and sleeping huts with separate compartments for each officer, and a complete issue of beds. A busy week was spent in re-organizing, and practically reconstituting the whole Battalion and replenishing the equipment, practically the whole of which had been lost in the Ypres battle.

When the Brigade moved into support on 30th September, the Battalion went to their old quarters at Goldfish Chateau for a week before relieving the 5th Warwicks in the trenches on the 7th. Two days later they were relieved by the Oxfords and went into the support line round Warwick Farm, but moved up to the line again the next night. The weather was bad and the enemy shelling was heavy and continuous. The casualties, however, were not serious, other ranks killed 16 and wounded 36, the greater number of which occurred by the explosion of a shell in the concrete dug-out used by the Headquarters Section. Having been originally constructed by the Germans, the entrance faced towards the enemy, and through this the shell entered. Of the 26 occupants 12 were killed and only one escaped unhurt· Another shell burst against the door of an adjoining dug-out occupied by the Headquarters officers, killing the Battalion Provost Sergeant (Walker), who had been a Corporal in the Bucks Battalion for 12 years, and had come out with them in March, 1915, and had served continuously abroad from that date, and under orders to return the next week.

On the night of the 12th, the Battalion was relieved by the Gloucesters and after two nights at Goldfish Chateau in support moved to Brandhoek No. 2 camp about a mile south of Poperinghe, and then to Mill Camp (Watou). During their stay here they discovered the 1st Bucks in camp about four miles away, but due to move the next day. A football match was at once arranged which was won by the 1st Bucks after a close struggle. The day was thoroughly enjoyed by all ranks and marked the cordial relations existing between the Battalions. The evening was damp but cheerful.

On the 17th, the Battalion continued to move towards Arras, where they arrived on the 24th, and went into Lichfield Camp, St. Nicholas. On the 26th they celebrated the fourth birthday of the Battalion. A long programme of sports filled the afternoon and the Battalion concert party, the "Black and Whites," provided an entertainment of much merit in the evening, the men's dinners were liberally supplemented with extras, and the officers dined together after the concert, the guests including Colonel Williams, who was then Town Major in Arras, Capt. G. Bowyer, who was with the 183rd Brigade as Staff Captain, and Capt Newbury, the Division Baths Officer, all old officers of the Battalion.

October and the greater part of November were spent at Arras in the Greenland Hill Sector ; much work was done on the trenches, etc., under the Royal Engineers. Raids were at first of almost nightly occurrence and were generally successful in entering the enemy lines, but as these were found to be held only by a few caretakers little could be done either in identification or "attrition," and with the absence of results raiding became less frequent.

On the 29th, the Battalion entrained for Bapaume, the 61st Division having been ordered to that area to relieve some of the troops of the 3rd Army under General Sir Julian Byng, after their forward push which had thrust a salient into the enemy line towards Cambrai till checked at Bourlon Wood. On arrival at Bapaume news was received that the enemy had counter attacked, and had achieved a substantial success against the portions of our line facing Gouzeaucourt. Motor "Busses" were waiting in the station yard and the Battalion was at once conveyed to Bertincourt, where they were joined at a late hour by their transport which had come by road from Arras.

On the 2nd December, the Battalion moved forward through Metz into support in the neighbourhood of the Hindenburg line, and went into the line in front of Villers Pluish with the Oxfords on the right and the Berks in support. Though the shelling here was heavy the trenches at La Vacquerie afforded good protection and casualties were few. There were plentiful signs of the retirement that had taken place over that ground. Two camps were standing, one in No Man's Land and one just outside the remains of the village of Villers Pluish, which had been abandoned in haste and contained much that came in handy for replacing deficiencies. Salvage naturally was carried out with much zest, when opportunity offered, and much merit was acquired for what was returned to store. On the 10th the Battalion went into support in Havrincourt Wood, and on the 22nd moved billets to near Lechelle, whence they were railed to Suzanne two days later.

Early in January, the 61st Division moved forward to its old line at St. Quentin. The Battalion marched from Suzanne to Vauvillers, remained there a few days and then marched to Nesle where they entrained to go up to the front line in the same sector as before.

During February it was found that the man power of the country was insufficient to maintain all the units that had been formed, and at the same time to provide for the expansion necessary in Special Arms, Tanks, Machine Gun Battalions, Heavy Artillery, and Aircraft. It was, therefore, decided to reduce all Infantry Brigades to three battalions, and to effect the reduction on a basis of the man power of the recruiting areas.

In the 61st Division six Infantry Battalions were abolished. The 182nd Brigade composed of the 5th, 6th, 7th and 8th Warwicks, lost three battalions. The 183rd Brigade, composed of 4th and 6th Gloucesters, and 7th and 8th Worcesters, lost two, only one battalion of each county being retained. In the 184th Brigade the 4th Oxfords, 4th R. Berks, 5th Gloucesters were retained, and the 2/1st Bucks Battalion marked for abolition.

The composition of the Division then became : 182nd Brigade, the 2/5th Warwicks, 2/4th Gloucesters and 2/7th Worcesters ; 183rd Brigade, 1st E. Lancs. (Regulars), 11th Suffolks (Service Battalion), 4th Northumberland Fusiliers (Territorials) ; 184th Brigade, 2/4th Oxfords and Bucks L.I. into which the Bucks Battalion was eventually absorbed, the 2/4th R. Berks and 2/5th Gloucesters.

The surplus units were detached as entrenching battalions behind the line until drafts were required for the surviving units of their county regiment.

On 22nd February, the 2nd Bucks marched to Germaine and thence to Herly (near Nesle) where they became the 25th Entrenching Battalion and were employed on the construction of a light railway. Having recently received drafts the Battalion was strong : 42 officers, 6 W.O.'s, 120 N.C.O.'s, and 637 other ranks. Lt.-Col. Muir had gone on a month's leave, Major Christie-Miller was attending the senior officers' course at Aldershot, and Captain Tubbs was in command of the battalion. On the 21st March, the great German offensive took place and the whole St. Quentin front gave way under the ernormous pressure of the masses concentrated against that area. The battalion was called upon to assist in stemming the rush and did good service in the defence of Nesle. During the subsequent ten days, during which Major K. Honeybun had joined and assumed the command, the Battalion was attached to the 61st Brigade 20th Division, and was involved in continuous fighting during the retreat, gaining special distinction at Le Quesnil, Demuin, and Hanguard. Their losses in killed and wounded during this time amounted to 9 officers and 150 other ranks.

At Quevanvillers the Battalion left the 20th Division and rejoined the 61st Division near Avesne, where, on 7th April, the men remaining were absorbed into the 2/4th Oxfords which had lost heavily in their gallant defence of Enghien Redoubt, and the line in front on the 21st March, and during the subsequent withdrawal.

The amalgamation was smoothly carried out. The two Battalions dovetailed together satisfactorily, each able to make up the deficiencies of the other ; the combination was carried out without friction and proved a great success. Regret there was doubtless amongst the Bucks men at losing their separate county individuality, but the less was absorbed by the greater and the esprit de corps of the Battalion mingled in that of the Regiment. Side by side the men of Bucks and Oxford added to the laurels already won by the 2/4th Battalion of the Oxfordshire and Buckinghamshire Light Infantry.

A List of the Officers who were killed in action, or died of wounds, or who were reported " missing" whilst serving with the Battalion and the dates of these casualties

†SEC.-LT. C. P. QUAYLE	15th June, 1916
†CAPT. H. CHURCH	19th July, 1916
†LT. C. P. PHIPPS	19th July, 1916
†LT. G. W. ATKINSON	19th July, 1916
†SEC.LT. R. B. HUDSON	19th July, 1916
SEC.-LT. F. R. PARKER (Wilts. R.)	19th July, 1916
SEC.-LT. H. R. N. BREWIN (Wilts. R.)	19th July, 1916
†LT. D. G. CHADWICK	20th July, 1916
SEC.LT. E. H. WALTERS (Manch. R.)	26th Sept., 1916
CAPT. P. H. H. BECK (Glouc. R.)	2nd April, 1917
CAPT. H. R. FOSTER	22nd August, 1917
LT. H. E. MOLLOY	22nd August, 1917
SEC.LT. W. R. GILL	22nd August, 1917
SEC.LT. W. E. ROLFE	22nd August, 1917
SEC.LT. C. R. TYSON	22nd August, 1917
†CAPT. J. E. S. WILSON, M.C. (R.A.M.C.)	23rd August, 1917
SEC.LT. S. A. C. GIBSON, M.C. (Wilts. R.)	26th August, 1917

A List of the Warrant Officers Non-Commissioned Officers and Men who lost their lives whilst serving with the Battalion

PTE. H. DAVIS (London)	10th June,	1916
L.-CPL. E. E. D. JONES (Kirkdale)	22nd June,	1916
PTE. P. A. ALDRIDGE (High Wycombe)	26th June,	1916
PTE. F. R. CASTLETON (Lowestoft)	,,	,,
PTE. L. V. RIVETT (Gt. Yarmouth)	,,	,,
CPL. C. PERKINS (Watford)	9th July,	1916
CPL. J. WHITEHEAD (Padbury)	10th July,	1916
PTE. H. PRATT (The-Lee)	,,	,,
PTE. R. BOYER (Fazakerley)	18th July,	1916
PTE. A. BURROWS (Buckingham)	,,	,,
PTE. A. T. BURROWS (Buckingham)	,,	,,
PTE. J. FRITH (Marlow)	,,	,,
PTE. G. GIBBS (West Wycombe)	,,	,,
SERGT.-MAJOR A. BROWN (The-Lee)	19th July,	1916
SERGT. J. C. CRUMP (High Wycombe)	,,	,,
SERGT. G. E. DAVIS (Marlow)	,,	,,
SERGT. A. H. EAST (High Wycombe)	,,	,,
SERGT. F. C. LANCE (High Wycombe)	,,	,,
SERGT. G. E. D. WOOD (Hunsdon)	,,	,,
CPL. E. C. BATTAMS (Bletchley)	,,	,,
CPL. A. V. FINCHER (Stantonbury)	,,	,,
CPL. A. OXLADE (High Wycombe)	,,	,,
L.-CPL. W. H. V. J. BRUCE (Chesham Bois)	,,	,,
L.-CPL. J. BURNARD (High Wycombe)	,,	,,
L.CPL. J. CASEMORE (Quainton)	,,	,,
L.-CPL. A. COOK (Buckingham)	,,	,,
L.-CPL. C. C. DELL (Wendover)	,,	,,
L.-CPL. A. EVANS (Hazlemere)	,,	,,
L.-CPL. W. J. HOLDOM (Winslow)	,,	,,
L.-CPL. W. JOHNSON (Slough)	,,	,,
L.-CPL. C. G. LUFF (Aylesbury)	,,	,,
L.-CPL. G. W. MANTRIPP (Lowestoft)	,,	,,
L.-CPL. W. C. PEARCE (Booker)	,,	,,
L.-CPL. E. SHARPE (The-Lee)	,,	,,
L.-CPL. A. F. STEVENS (Windsor)	,,	,,
L.-CPL. G. SYMONDS (Aston Clinton)	,,	,,
L.-CPL. A. THORPE (Buckingham)	,,	,,

L.-CPL. A. WALKER (West Wycombe) ..	19th July,	1916
L.-CPL. S. WOOD (Oulton Broad) ..	,,	,,
L.-CPL. C. H. WRIGHT (Lowestoft) ..	,,	,,
PTE. A. ALDRIDGE (High Wycombe) ..	,,	,,
PTE. F. H. ANDREWS (Stantonbury) ..	,,	,,
PTE. S. H. AVIS (Colnbrook)	,,	,,
PTE. H. BALDWIN (Weybridge)	,,	,,
PTE. F. W. BARKAWAY (Lowestoft) ..	,,	,,
PTE. H. BENNETT (Uxbridge)	,,	,,
PTE. S. A. BIRCH (Aston Clinton) ..	,,	,,
PTE. J. R. BOND (Buckingham)	,,	,,
PTE. W. BONE (Buckland)	,,	,,
PTE. J. L. BOWIE (Aberdeen)	,,	,,
PTE. A. BRASSINGTON (Uttoxeter) ..	,,	,,
PTE. E. BROWN (Slough)	,,	,,
PTE. J. BUNCE (Haddenham)	,,	,,
PTE. J. BUTT (Blandford)	,,	,,
PTE. A. G. CARTER (High Wycombe) ..	,,	,,
PTE. R. CARTER (High Wycombe) ..	,,	,,
PTE. G. E. CARVER (Oulton Broad) ..	,,	,,
PTE. G. A. CASTLE (Warwick)	,,	,,
PTE. E. A. P. CLARKE (Weston Turville)	,,	,,
PTE. G. COLEMAN (Chippenham)	,,	,, .
PTE. G. COOK (Aylesbury)	,,	,,
PTE. H. J. COOK (Bruton)	,,	,,
PTE. T. A. COX (Waddesdon)	,,	,,
PTE. F. CRUTCHFIELD (High Wycombe)	,,	,,
PTE. A. DAVIS (High Wycombe)	,,	,,
PTE. T. DAVENEY (Wooburn Green) ..	,,	,,
PTE. S. DWIGHT (The-Lee)	,,	,,
PTE. E. H. FOWLER (Waddesdon) ..	,,	,,
PTE. H. R. GIBSON (Winslow)	,,	,,
PTE. W. GRAY (High Wycombe)	,,	,,
PTE. E. W. GROVES (Eton)	,,	,,
PTE. R. W. GUNTRIP (Stantonbury) ..	,,	,,
PTE. H. HARDING (The-Lee)	,,	,,
PTE. A. J. HARRIS (Lane End)	,,	,,
PTE. S. HENLEY (North Marston) ..	,,	,,
PTE. A. HILL (Chesham Bois)	,,	,,
PTE. F. S. HODGSON (Wolverton) ..	,,	,,

PTE. H. W. HOGSTON (Whitchurch) ..	19th July 1916
PTE. W. HOLT (Wootton Park)	,, ,,
PTE. C. J. HUMPHREY (High Wycombe)	,, ,,
PTE. A. G. JARVIS (Aylesbury)	,, ,,
PTE. O. L. JOHNS (Bootle)	,, ,,
PTE. J. W. JONES (Bow)	,, ,,
PTE. T. E. KING (Reading)	,, ,,
PTE. J. KIPPING (Slough)	,, ,,
PTE. W. KNIGHTS (Beccles)	,, ,,
PTE. E. LEWIS (High Wycombe) ..	,, ,,
PTE. F. W. LINE (Sharnbrook)	,, ,,
PTE. A. MCCLEMENTS (Liverpool) ..	,, ,,
PTE. R. MARSHALL (Dumfries)	,, ,,
PTE. R. V. MARSLEN (Merton Park) ..	,, ,,
PTE. A. H. MORRIS (Aylesbury)	,, ,,
PTE. A. W. MORRIS (The-Lee)	,, ,,
PTE. C. R. MUNDAY (Aylesbury)	,, ,,
PTE. F. H. NEWSON (Framlingham) ..	,, ,,
PTE. T. E. PARKER (Sydenham)	,, ,,
PTE. E. PAYNE (Beaconsfield)	,, ,,
PTE. J. W. PERRY (Kirkdale)	,, ,,
PTE. C. G. PLOWMAN (Slough)	,, ,,
PTE. G. E. PRATT (Slough)	,, ,,
PTE. H. PRENTICE (Tring)	,, ,,
PTE. P. PRICE (The-Lee)	,, ,,
PTE. H. T. PRICE (North Marston) ..	,, ,,
PTE. G. E. SAVIN (Marlow)	,, ,,
PTE. A. SAYELL (Ford)	,, ,,
PTE. G. SEXTON (West Wycombe) ..	,, ,,
PTE. J. W. SIMMONDS (Marlow)	,, ,,
PTE. R. SINCLAIR (West Norwood) ..	,, ,,
PTE. H. SMITH (Bierton)	,, ,,
PTE. J. T. SOULL (Swindon)	,, ,,
PTE. G. C. STONE (High Wycombe) ..	,, ,,
PTE. F. TAVENER (Ivinghoe Aston) ..	,, ,,
PTE. S. TAYLOR (Haddenham)	,, ,,
PTE. T. TAYLOR (Slough)	,, ,,
PTE. S. A. S. THOMAS (Brynnially) ..	,, ,,
PTE. H. TOMES (East Claydon)	,, ,,
PTE. W. T. UPSON (East Ham)	,, ,,

PTE. B. W. G. WARR (Bletchley)	19th July, 1916
PTE. J. WHITE (Hanslope)	,, ,,
PTE. R. J. WILLIAMS (Buckingham)	,, ,,
PTE. F. T. WILLIS (Hanslope)	,, ,,
PTE. S. WOOD (Wendover)	,, ,,
SERGT.-MAJOR R. W. BROWN (The-Lee)	20th July, 1916
PTE. E. DURRANT (East Knoyle)	,, ,,
PTE. S. F. PHILLIPS (Adstock)	,, ,,
PTE. W. A. WALLACE (Aylesbury)	,, ,,
SERGT. C. V. AUSTIN (Marlow)	22nd July, 1916
PTE. T. S. HUGHES (Liverpool)	,, ,,
PTE. F. A. MALCOLM (Long Acre)	,, ,,
PTE. A. L. DOYLE (Liverpool)	24th July, 1916
PTE. S. W. JEFFS (Aston Abbots)	,, ,,
PTE. T. H. LAMBOURNE (High Wycombe)	,, ,,
PTE. J. COX (Bletchley)	25th July, 1916
PTE. S. DAMANT (Marlow)	,, ,,
PTE. F. DIMMOCK (Gt. Missenden)	,, ,,
PTE. C. C. HAVERLEY (Bradenham)	26th July, 1916
PTE. L. JOHNSTON (Streatham)	13th August, 1916
PTE. W. SHAW (Aylesbury)	18th August, 1916
PTE. G. HANCE (Tring)	26th August, 1916
CPL. J. E. TAPPER (Westbury)	29th August, 1916
L.-CPL. E. S. HAYWARD (Colnbrook)	31st August, 1916
SERGT. W. A. MEAD (Stewkley)	8th September, 1916
L.-CPL. R. HARRALL (High Wycombe)	,, ,,
PTE. J. S. LITCHFIELD (Bletchley)	,, ,,
PTE. H. J. WEAVER (Weymouth)	,, ,,
PTE. J. E. G. DAVIES (Pembroke Dock)	14th October, 1916
SERGT. J. CRANE (Woking)	15th October, 1916
PTE. J. MORRIS (High Wycombe)	22nd October, 1916
PTE. L. RODWELL (Waddesdon)	,, ,,
L.-CPL. J. RODWELL (Chalvey)	22nd November, 1916
L.-CPL. J. DUBERY (Stone)	25th November, 1916
PTE. J. R. BROOKS (Newport Pagnell)	,, ,,
PTE. E. C. BRYANT, (Wetherden)	,, ,,
PTE. G. MITCHELL (Camborne)	,, ,,
L.-CPL. J. BRYANT (Maids Moreton)	28th November, 1916
PTE. R. COLLINS (High Wycombe)	30th November, 1916
PTE. C. GOULD (Wareham)	,, ,,

PTE. J. WILKINS (Gt. Missenden) ..	30th November, 1916
PTE. F. HORROCKS (Edge Hill) ..	1st December, 1916
CPL. A. E. TOFIELD (Aylesbury) ..	9th December, 1916
PTE. G. F. HALL (Lechdale)	2nd January, 1917
PTE. R. LAMBERT (Llanelly) ..	18th January, 1917
PTE. G. E. LESLIE (Walgrave ..	28th February, 1917
PTE. S. STREET (Arlesey)	,, ,,
L.-CPL. H. C. COCKLE (Depden)	2nd March, 1917
PTE. C. P. ACKERMAN (Slough)	,, ,,
PTE. W. L. HARTLEY (Doncaster) ..	12th March, 1917
CPL. E. AXTELL (Weston Turville) ..	15th March, 1917
PTE. A. RUTLAND (The-Lee)	27th March, 1917
PTE. W. HUCKLE (Newport Pagnell) ..	31st March, 1917
SERGT. J. BLACKWELL (High Wycombe)	2nd April, 1917
SERGT. R. HESELTINE (Manchester) ..	,, ,,
PTE. A. LOOKER (Farnham Common) ..	,, ,,
PTE. T. CRADDOCK (Smethwick)	,, ,,
PTE. C. CURRELL (Lacey Green)	,, ,,
PTE. J. KEATING (Liverpool)	,, ,,
PTE. J. LONGLAND (Olney)	,, ,,
PTE. W. MEAD (Haversham)..	,, ,,
PTE. C. W. A. STAMMERS (Aylesbury)..	,, ,,
PTE. S. J. MORRIS (Bletchley)	19th April, 1917
PTE. H. T. JACKSON (Aylesbury) ..	22nd April, 1917
PTE. P. RIDGELEY (Princes Risborough)	,, ,,
CPL. C. F. HOPCRAFT (Weedon)	26th April, 1917
PTE. J. USHER (Cookham Dean)	27th April, 1917
PTE. C. E. GAIR (Leicester)	5th June, 1917
PTE. A. WOODS (Birmingham)	,, ,,
SERGT. W. H. CROSS (Stony Stratford)	6th June, 1917
PTE. H. C. CLARK (Henley)	9th June, 1917
PTE. W. H. MILLER (Witney)	14th July, 1917
PTE. E. G. FYNN (Bristol)	14th August, 1917
PTE. H. F. WHEELER (Aylesbury) ..	21st August, 1917
SGT.-MAJ. W. P. CLARKE (Halesworth)..	22nd August, 1917
SERGT. W. H. ANSTEY (Winslow) ..	,, ,,
SERGT. H. CARTER (Waddesdon)	,, ,,
SERGT. C. E. JOHNSON (Aylesbury) ..	,, ,,
SERGT. H. STALLWOOD (High Wycombe)	,, ,,
SERGT. A. WALKER (Winslow)	,, ,,

SERGT. A. V. WOODLEY (High Wycombe) 22nd August, 1917
CPL. A. CLARK (Wolverton) .. .. .. ,, ,,
L.-CPL. J. ADNITT (Chesham) .. .. ,, ,,
L-CPL. R. J. G. BIRD (Waddesdon) .. ,, ,,
L.-CPL. H. BISWELL (Waddesdon) .. ,, ,,
L.-CPL. A. W. CREW (Marlow) .. .. ,, ,,
L.-CPL. N. CULLEY (Wycombe Marsh) ,, ,,
L.-CPL. F. G. ELKINS (Lindford) .. .. ,, ,,
L.-CPL. W. G. LITTLEWOOD (Oulton Broad) ,, ,,
L.CPL. A. J. NEWMAN (Aylesbury) .. ,, ,,
L.-CPL. G. H. SMITH (Helston) .. .. ,, ,,
L.-CPL. W. SMITH (Bampton) .. .. ,, ,,
L.-CPL. R. T. TACK (Windsor) .. .. ,, ,,
L.-CPL. R. R. WOODLAND (Homerton) ,, ,,
PTE. M. J. ABBOTT (Lane End) .. .. ,, ,,
PTE. J. ANDREWS (Southampton) .. ,, ,,
PTE. J. BARNETT (London) .. .. .. ,, ,,
PTE. F. BECKETT (Woughton Green) .. ,, ,,
PTE. F. C. P. BENNETT (Southampton) ,, ,,
PTE. S. BOWLER (High Wycombe) .. ,, ,,
PTE. F. BRAVINGTON (High Wycombe) ,, ,,
PTE. E. H. BROWN (Wallington) .. .. ,, ,,
PTE. F. A. BROWN (Beccles) .. .. ,, ,,
PTE. J. H. BURLEY (Birmingham) .. ,, ,,
PTE. G. BURNHAM (Marlow) .. .. .. ,, ,,
PTE. A. CARROD (Slough) .. .. .. ,, ,,
PTE. G. J. CASTLE (Amersham) .. .. ,, ,,
PTE. F. J. CHAPMAN (Lye Green) .. ,, ,,
PTE. J. CHINNOCK (Redruth) .. .. ,, ,,
PTE. A. F. COLEMAN (Aylesbury) .. ,, ,,
PTE. F. C. G. COLES (Bruton) .. .. ,, ,,
PTE. P. F. COLLCUTT (Oxford) .. .. ,, ,,
PTE. H. O. COLLINS (Southampton) .. ,, ,,
PTE. G. T. COOLEY (Fetsworth) .. .. ,, ,,
PTE. A. COX (Newton Longville) .. .. ,, ,,
PTE. R. W. CREW (Marlow) .. .. .. ,, ,,
PTE. H. CRIPPS (Waddesdon) .. .. ,, ,,
PTE. A. CUNNINGTON (Titchencote) .. ,, ,,
PTE. T. J. DAW (High Wycombe) .. ,, ,,
PTE. A. V. DREWITT (Wolvercote) .. ,, ,,

PTE. W. J. EASDEN (High Wycombe)	22nd August, 1917
PTE. H. J. EDWARDS (Andover)	,, ,,
PTE. W. C. EVANS (Hanslope)	,, ,,
PTE. F. W. FESSEY (Wolverton)	,, ,,
PTE. G. FREEMANTLE (Bournemouth)	,, ,,
PTE. W. FLETCHER (High Wycombe)	,, ,,
PTE. F. GIBBS (Aylesbury)	,, ,,
PTE. F. W. GIBBS (High Wycombe)	,, ,,
PTE. S. B. GOODWIN (Oundle)	,, ,,
PTE. H. GREEN (Witney)	,, ,,
PTE. C. HAWKEN (Mawgan)	,, ,,
PTE. H. E. HAYNES (Kidlington)	,, ,,
PTE. C. H. HIGGOTT (High Wycombe)	,, ,,
PTE. F. W. HIGGS (Datchet)	,, ,,
PTE. E. HODGKINSON (High Wycombe)	,, ,,
PTE. G. HOOD (Birmingham)	,, ,,
PTE. F. J. HOOPER (Portland)	,, ,,
PTE. E. HUNT (Blandford)	,,
PTE. H. JEFFS (Weedon)	,, ,,
PTE. J. R. JILLIANS (Slough)	,, ,,
PTE. W. T. KENWARD (Alton)	,, ,,
PTE. T. KINGHAM (Ford)	,, ,,
PTE. A. LAVENDER (Mile End)	,, ,,
PTE. T. LAWLOR (Birmingham)	,, ,,
PTE. A. LOTSKY (Whitechapel)	,, ,,
PTE. R. G. LOWE (Cowley)	,, ,,
PTE. A. J. LUCAS (Portsmouth)	,, ,,
PTE. E. LYNCH (Uttoxeter)	,, ,,
PTE. J. A. LYNCH (Forest Gate)	,, ,,
PTE. A. MERRYWEATHER (Basingstoke)	,, ,,
PTE. F. MORLEY (Chard)	,, ,,
PTE. E. W. MOSELEY (Eton)	,, ,,
PTE. J. P. OAK (Aldershot)	,, ,,
PTE. E. J. PACE (Dalston)	,, ,,
PTE. W. J. PARSONS (Wheatley)	,, ,,
PTE. F. E. PAULLEY (Dorchester)	,, ,,
PTE. F. J. PAYNE (Lostwithiel)	,, ,,
PTE. J. E. PLUMRIDGE (Stokenchurch)	,, ,,
PTE. H. C. PYNE (Southampton)	,, ,,
PTE. W. J. READ (Bournemouth)	,, ,,

PTE. T. A. R. ROBINSON (Wolverton) . 22nd August, 1917
PTE. E. SAUNDERS (Ryde) .. .. .. ,, ,,
PTE. P. G. SAUNDERS (Oxford) .. .. ,, ,,
PTE. H. R. SEYMOUR (Watlington) .. ,, ,,
PTE. H. SHARP (Dunton) .. .. .. ,, ,,
PTE. F. H. SHELDON (Handsworth) .. ,, ,,
PTE. W. SLATTER (Coombe) .. .. .. ,
PTE. C. H. SLOCOMBE (Bristol) .. .. ,, ,,
PTE. G. A. SMITH (Christchurch) .. .. ,, ,,
PTE. W. B. SOUSTER (Bletchley) .. .. ,, ,,
PTE. F. S. STERRY (Bristol) .. .. .. ,, ,,
PTE. S. STONEHILL (Waddesdon) .. ,, ,,
PTE. D. STURGESS (Hazlemere) .. .. ,, ,,
PTE. R. TERRY (Southampton) .. .. ,, ,,
PTE. R. TIMBERLAKE (High Wycombe) ,, ,,
PTE. J. TODD (Aylesbury) .. .. .. ,, ,,
PTE. H. A. VICKERY (Aylesbury).. .. ,, ,,
PTE. E. WATERS (Cheddington) .. .. ,, ,,
PTE. A. WATKINS (High Wycombe) .. ,, ,,
PTE. W. WATTS (Birmingham) .. .. ,, ,,
PTE. E. A. WEAVER (Witney) .. .. ,, ,,
PTE. A. T. WEST (Aylesbury) .. .. ,, ,,
PTE. F. J. WHITE (Portland) .. .. ,, ,,
PTE. J. W. WHITING (Stanton St. Johns) ,, ,,
PTE. J. D. WILKINSON (Blandford) .. ,, ,,
PTE. D. WILSON (Brookfields) .. .. ,, ,,
PTE. H. WILSON (Haddenham) .. .. ,, ,,
PTE. A. WORRELL (Buckland Wharf) .. ,, ,,
PTE. C. G. WRIGHT (Oxford).. .. .. ,, ,,
PTE. W. THORPE (Waddesdon) .. .. 23rd August, 1917
PTE. A. E. HORNE (Bourne End) .. 24th August, 1917
PTE. J. L. D. DELBRIDGE (Cubert) .. 25th August, 1917
PTE. G. W. BARTLETT (Chipping Norton) 26th August, 1917
PTE. A. J. GRAY (Oxford) .. .. 2nd September, 1917
PTE. A. KING (Leytonstone) .. ,, ,,
PTE. F. C. LAWRENCE (Old Swindon) ,, ,,
PTE. H. STEVENS (Marlow) .. .. ,, ,,
PTE. A. H. GREEN (Oxford) .. .. 8th September, 1917
PTE. G. A. GROVES (Chiswick) .. ,, ,,
PTE. A. MUNDAY (Cuddington) .. ,, ,,

PTE. T. H. PINFIELD (Dunster) ..	8th September, 1917
PTE. W. H. TANDY (Birmingham)	,, ,,
PTE. W. J. BURTON (Luton) ..	9th September, 1917
PTE. J. R. GREEN (Iver Heath) ..	11th September, 1917
PTE. T. HEATH (Bournemouth) ..	,, ,,
PTE. A. J. HERBERT (Hanslope) ..	,, ,,
PTE F. J. HICKS (Langley)	,, ,,
PTE. H. SEARS (Watford)	,, ,,
PTE. A. TAYLOR (Aston)	,, ,,
PTE. G. F. WHITE (Southampton)..	,, ,,
PTE. G. F. YOUERS (High Wycombe)	,, ,,
PTE. T. C. INGRAM (Oxford) ..	14th September, 1917
PTE. J. A. ELLIOTT (Whitstone) ..	22nd October, 1917
PTE. F. FREEMAN (Christchurch)	15th November, 1917
CPL. T. A. CLEE (Slough)	23rd November, 1917
PTE. P. J. CRITCHLEY (Plymouth)	6th December, 1917
PTE. W. H. POLMEAR (Truro) ..	,, ,,
PTE. J. WHITE (Wycombe Marsh) ..	10th March, 1918
L.-CPL. R. PIKE (Yeovil)	21st March, 1918
PTE. G. BELCHER (Banbury).. ..	,, ,,
PTE. S. G. NORTON (Maidenhead) ..	,, ,,
L.-CPL. F. BROOKS (High Wycombe) ..	22nd March, 1918
PTE. A. J. LINTON (Blandford)	,, ,,
PTE. A. J. WILLIS (Liverpool)	,, ,,
PTE. T. BATTEN (Chard)	23rd March, 1918
PTE. L. A. CATERER (Aylesbury) ..	,, ,,
PTE. T. A. DRUCE (Birmingham) ..	,, ,,
PTE. V. LONGMAN (Armborne)	,, ,,
PTE. S. MINTON (Birmingham)	,, ,,
PTE. E. SOPER (Wareham)	,, ,,
PTE. G. WOOLHEAD (Wing)	,, ,,
PTE. W. LAWRENCE (Chalfont St. Giles)	25th March, 1918
PTE. H. H. PRICE (Westgate-on-Sea) ..	,, ,,
PTE. J. H. LAMBOURNE (North Marston)	27th March, 1918
PTE. C. A. STANLEY (Aylesbury)	29th March, 1918
PTE. W. FRAMPTON (Southampton) ..	30th March, 1918
PTE. W. BARDEN (Fenny Stratford) ..	31st March, 1918
PTE. E. HICKS (Newton Purcell)	,, ,,
PTE. T. PRITCHARD (High Wycombe) .	,, ,,
PTE. F. T. WALKER (High Wycombe)..	,, ,,
PTE. T. W. BUTLER (Buckingham) ..	1st April, 1918

A List of the Officers who gained distinctions whilst serving with the Battalion

---

† LT.-COLONEL H. M. WILLIAMS, D.L., V.D.
Mentioned in Dispatches   1st January, 1917

LT.-COL. J. B. MUIR (R. High.)
The Distinguished Service Order   18th October, 1917
Mentioned in Dispatches   24th May, 1917
Mentioned in Dispatches   7th November, 1917

† MAJOR G. CHRISTIE-MILLER
The Military Cross   1st January, 1918
Mentioned in Dispatches   24th May, 1917

* † CAPT. I. STEWART-LIBERTY
The Military Cross   23rd August, 1916
" He displayed complete disregard of personal danger and by his fine example under heavy fire gave great encouragement to his men. He kept them together in the assault under heavy machine-gun fire and led them to the enemy's trenches. He was severely wounded."

* † CAPT. J. E. S. WILSON (R.A.M.C.)
The Military Cross   23rd August, 1916
" He went up to the front line from his Aid Post through a very heavy barrage, in order to assist the wounded. By his pluck and skill he undoubtedly saved many lives. He afterwards controlled the evacuation of the casualties under heavy fire."

He served continuously with the Battalion until the 23rd August, 1917, when he died of wounds received the day before.

* † SEC.-LT. A. H. PHILLIPS
The Military Cross   23rd August, 1916
" He went out into ' No Man's Land ' to reconnoitre and rally men under very heavy shrapnel and machine-gun fire. He showed great coolness and brought back valuable information."

* † SEC.-LT. B. H. DRAKES (E. Yorks. R.)
The Military Cross   23rd August, 1916
"He commanded the leading platoon of the assault with great dash, and, though his thumb was blown off early in the advance, he stuck to his command till again wounded in the leg after he had reached the enemy's lines."

† CAPT. and ADJT. G. E. W. BOWYER
The Military Cross   1st January, 1917

* † CAPT. V. W. H. RANGER
The Military Cross   1st January, 1917

* SEC.-LT. S. A. C. GIBSON (Wilts. R.)
The Military Cross   25th August, 1917
"For conspicuous gallantry and devotion to duty in an attack on the enemy's position. Although wounded on four separate occasions, he continued to lead his company until incapacitated by a serious wound in the back. By his gallant conduct and personal example he got them through to their objective under extremely heavy rifle and machine-gun fire from front and flanks."

He died of wounds a few hours after hearing of the distinction he had won.

CAPT. L. F. BUTTFIELD
The Military Cross   18th October, 1917
"In an attack when his company officers had become casualties he took command, re-organized the men, and consolidated the position won, and held the line until relieved. He showed complete disregard for personal safety, and his good leading contributed largely to the success of the attack."

* SEC.-LT. C. V. HILL
The Military Cross   18th October, 1917
"He led his platoon with the utmost gallantry on a concrete machine-gun emplacement, which he captured, killing three of the enemy. Being wounded, he directed the fire of his platoon from the top of the gun emplacement on to another enemy machine-gun, which he captured. His cheerfulness and courage under heavy fire had a splendid effect on his men."

* SEC.-LT. W. H. PETRIE (Manch. R.)
The Military Cross   18th October, 1917

"During the assembly for the attack he showed great coolness in forming up his platoon under heavy shell fire, and, though blown up by a shell before the attack began, he led his platoon forward until he was badly wounded. He then continued to encourage his men, setting a magnificent example of coolness and pluck throughout."

† CAPT. W. A. GREENE (Special Appt.)
The Military Cross   1st January, 1918
Croix de Guerre (French)   September, 1917
Corona d'Italia   April, 1918

* SEC.-LT. F. ROBERTS
The Military Cross   22nd April, 1918

"When in charge of a fighting patrol he was heavily fired on and rushed by a party of the enemy forty strong. By his coolness and gallant example he re-organized his party, engaged the enemy in a hand-to-hand struggle and drove them off. With four other ranks he covered the successful withdrawal of the remainder of the patrol, who carried back three of the four casualties. He then collected a stretcher party and returned to the remaining wounded man, who was safely brought in to our lines. By his cool determination, initiative, and fine fighting spirit he kept his patrol together, and broke up an enemy attempt on one of our isolated posts."

SEC.-LT. S. F. KEMP
The Military Cross   11th May, 1918

"He made several daring reconnaissances, penetrating far into the enemy's country, and bringing back information of the greatest value. He displayed a fine example of gallantry and disregard of personal danger."

* † CAPT. F. R. FLOYD (Devon R.)
The Military Cross   3rd June, 1918

† CAPT. and ADJT. R. F. SYMONDS
Croix de Guerre (Belgian)   December, 1917

† CAPT. A. TUBBS
Mentioned in Dispatches   11th November, 1917

A List of the Non-Commissioned Officers and Men who gained distinctions whilst serving with the Battalion

CPL. F. GURNEY (Aylesbury)
The Distinguished Conduct Medal 23rd August, 1916

" For conspicuous gallantry during operations. He showed the greatest courage and promptness in repairing some apparatus which had been hit by an enemy shell. He also led a bombing party in the assault with great courage."

R. SERGT.-MAJOR E. JONES (High Wycombe)
The Distinguished Conduct Medal 15th February, 1917

" For conspicuous gallantry in action. He displayed great courage and initiative in re-organizing the battalion during a heavy bombardment. He has at all times set a splendid example."

Mentioned in Dispatches 24th May, 1917

SERGT.-MAJOR J. H. ROLFE (Waddesdon)
The Distinguished Conduct Medal 4th June, 1917

" For conspicuous gallantry and devotion to duty. He has consistently performed good work in obtaining valuable information during raids, and has set a fine example at all times."

SERGT.-MAJOR T. HEARN (Aylesbury)
The Distinguished Conduct Medal 18th June, 1917

" For conspicuous gallantry and devotion to duty. He rendered invaluable assistance to his officer in re-organizing the company and superintending the consolidation of the position."

SERGT. W. P. CLARKE (Halesworth)
The Distinguished Conduct Medal 18th July, 1917

" For conspicuous gallantry and devotion to duty. On observing a party of the enemy attempting to get through our outpost lines, he, on his own iniative, took two men and advanced on the enemy and attacked them. By means of bombs and rifle fire he dispersed a party greatly superior in numbers."

CPL. A. BRAWN (Newport Pagnell)
The Distinguished Conduct Medal   18th July, 1917

"For conspicuous gallantry and devotion to duty. A party of the enemy had advanced and occupied a position close to his post. He at once left his post with his bombers, and with great gallantry attacked and dispersed a superior force."

L.-CPL. S. L. ABRAHAMS (London)
The Distinguished Conduct Medal   22nd October, 1917

"For conspicuous gallantry and devotion to duty as runner during an attack. When his platoon commander was wounded he carried him to a place of safety, under intense machine-gun fire. He returned to the platoon, and, finding it without a leader, took command and led it in a most gallant manner to its objective. He then went to Battalion Headquarters with important information through an intense barrage, and, having handed over his platoon to a supporting company, continued his duties as runner, under heavy fire. He showed the greatest initiative and courage on this and several occasions."

SERGT. H. J. HURST (Wolverton)
The Distinguished Conduct Medal   22nd October, 1917

"For conspicuous gallantry and devotion to duty in an attack. He was in command of a platoon, and, though wounded, he continued to lead them, gained his objective, and consolidated the position. He then made untiring efforts to bring in wounded, and saved the lives of an officer and several men. He inspired all his men by his energy and leadership."

SERGT. S. SMITH (Aston Abbotts)
The Distingiushed Conduct Medal   22nd October, 1917

"For conspicuous gallantry and devotion to duty. When all officers had become casualties except the company commander, he was of the greatest assistance to the latter in going from one part of the line to another and re-organizing the platoons under very heavy shell and machine-gun fire. During the whole operation he displayed tireless energy and courage, which inspired the men with confidence.

SERGT.-MAJOR W. T. ALLOWAY (Marlow)
The Distinguished Conduct Medal　　　1st January, 1918
"For conspicuous gallantry and devotion to duty. When his company trench had been completely destroyed by shell fire he re-organized the company and set a magnificent example of soldierly bearing. He has consistently rendered the utmost assistance to his company commander."

SERGT.-MAJOR J. PETTY (Aylesbury)
The Military Medal　　　21st September, 1916

CPL. T. OLDROYD (High Wycombe)
The Military Medal　　　21st September, 1916

CPL. R. HAYERS (Beaconsfield)
The Military Medal　　　21st September, 1916

L.-CPL. R. G. FRANCKLOW (Wolverton)
The Military Medal　　　21st September, 1916

PTE. W. SANDERS (Wolverton)
The Military Medal　　　21st September, 1916
Bar to The Military Medal　　　28th January, 1918
2nd Bar to The Military Medal　　　29th April, 1918

SERGT. O. BALDWIN (Weybridge)
The Military Medal　　　26th May, 1917

CPL. E. WINDSOR (Loudwater)
The Military Medal　　　9th July, 1917

L.-CPL. F. BAILEY (Aylesbury)
The Military Medal　　　2nd November, 1917

PTE. T. E. BUGGINS (Charlbury)
The Military Medal　　　2nd November, 1917

L.-CPL. B. LANGSTON (Wycombe Marsh)
The Military Medal　　　2nd November, 1917

PTE. W. H. POLMEAR (Truro)
The Military Medal　　　2nd November, 1917

PTE. A. WALKER (Bletchley)
The Military Medal   2nd November, 1917

SERGT. A. J. UNDERWOOD (Simpson)
The Military Medal   2nd November, 1917

CPL. H. WILLINGHAM (Hanslope)
The Military Medal   2nd November, 1917

CPL. S. AXTELL (Chalvey)
The Military Medal   23rd February, 1918

CPL. R. BIGGS (High Wycombe)
The Military Medal   23rd February, 1918

CPL. E. P. HASKINS (Bristol)
The Military Medal   29th April, 1918

PTE. H. G. BROOKS (Aylesbury)
The Military Medal   29th April, 1918

QM.-SERGT. S. F. BEECHEY (Stone)
The Meritorious Service Medal   4th June, 1918

SERGT. E. E. HIGGINS (Windsor)
The Meritorious Service Medal   4th June, 1918

SERGT. C. C. THORNE (Whitchurch)
The Meritorious Service Medal   4th June, 1918

SERGT. J. F. MACMAHON (Birmingham)
(Brigade Staff)
The Meritorious Service Medal   4th June, 1918

CPL. C. W. GRACE (High Wycombe)
Croix de Guerre (Belgian)   12th July, 1918

R.QM.-SERGT. G. F. GREAVES (Gerrards Cross)
Mentioned in Dispatches   21st December, 1917

QM.-SERGT. W. F. TAYLOR (Bradwell)
Mentioned in Dispatches   21st December, 1917

SERGT. W. LORD (High Wycombe)
Mentioned in Dispatches   7th April, 1918

A List of the other Officers who served with the Battalion overseas and their rank at the time of such service

     † MAJOR H. L. C. BARRETT
     † CAPT. H. S. G. BUCKMASTER
* † CAPT. G. C. STEVENS
     † CAPT. W. A. CUMMINS
* † QM. and HON. CAPT. D. WALLER
     † LT. E. M. LETTS
     † LT. P. E. WELLS
     † LT. E. W. LONG
     † LT. J. B. QUAYLE
* * † LT. A. T. PITCHER
* † SEC.-LT. J. S. RUTHERFORD
     † LT. A. A. IONIDES (Devon R.)
* * † SEC.-LT. T. J. RELF (Devon R.)
* † SEC.-LT. J. WARD (E. Yorks. R.)
     † LT. F. D. OLLARD
* † LT. T. S. MARKHAM (Hunts. R.)
     † CAPT. THE REV. J. R. FOSTER (C.F.)
     LT. C. R. CLUTSOM (Wilts. R.)
* LT. N. V. KENT (Wilts. R.)
* SEC.-LT. H. G. BADDELEY (Wilts. R.)
* SEC.-LT. A. J. SMEE (Wilts. R.)
     † SEC.-LT. G. D'A. W. OLIVER (Wilts. R.)
     SEC.-LT. S. MYLIUS (Manch. R.)
     SEC.-LT. F. B. ALLEN (Manch. R.)
     SEC.-LT. C. FOY (Manch. R.)
* SEC.-LT. J. KIRK (Manch. R.)
     SEC.-LT. G. THORLEY (Manch. R.)
* SEC.-LT. E. R. STREAT (Manch. R.)
     LT. B. J. NEWBURY
     † LT. R. G. HUGHES
     SEC.LT. L. ST. J. REEVE
     LT. H. S. STERN (Manch. R.)
     SEC.-LT. W. GIBBONS (Manch. R.)
     SEC.-LT. C. K. DEAKIN (Manch. R.)
     SEC.-LT. C. C. HORNER (Manch. R.)

* SEC.-LT. H. R. METCALFE (Manch. R.)
  SEC.-LT. G. A. ROYLE (Manch. R.)
  LT. J. M. ROLLESTON
* * CAPT. A. T. A. WILKINS
  SEC.-LT. R. THOMAS
  SEC.-LT. G. E. CARLOSS
  SEC.-LT. L. G. E. RAMAGE
  SEC.-LT. A. N. ELLISON
  CAPT. H. M. TYLER (R. Sussex R.)
  LT. G. L. TROUTBECK
  QM. and HON.-LT. W. H. GREEN
† SEC.-LT. P. STEED
  CAPT. J. P. BALSON (R. Berks. R.)
  MAJOR K. HUNNYBUN (Hunts. R.)
  CAPT. J. STANLEY (Hunts. R.)
  SEC.-LT. W. A. H. GOODMAN, (Hunts. R.)
  CAPT. J. A. RENNIE (R.A.M.C.)
  SEC.-LT. M. G. BEST (E. Surrey R.)
* SEC.-LT. F. KEYES (E. Surrey R.)
  LT. F. T. YOUNG (E. Kent R.)
  SEC.-LT. T. G. L. HARRIS
  SEC.-LT. E. D. G. HARRIES
  SEC.-LT. F. V. PONDER
  SEC.-LT. E. J. MCANSH
  SEC.-LT. H. T. L. DIBBEN (R.W. Kent R.)
* SEC.-LT. A. V. CURTICE
* SEC.-LT. J. M. SCOTT (R.W. Kent R.)
* SEC.-LT. A. DISHINGTON (R.W. Kent R.)
  SEC.-LT. T. LODGE (Oxf. & Bucks. Lt. Infty.)
  SEC.-LT. F. W. TAYLOR (Oxf. & Bucks. Lt. Infty.)
  SEC.-LT. P. KELSEY (Oxf. & Bucks. Lt. Infty.)
  SEC.-LT. D. A. MARTIN (Oxf. & Bucks. Lt. Infty.)
  SEC.-LT. C. F. BEESON (Oxf. & Bucks. Lt. Infty.)
* SEC.-LT. F. PRIEST (Oxf. & Bucks. Lt. Infty.)
  SEC.-LT. T. S. R. BOASE (Oxf. & Bucks. Lt. Infty.)
  SEC.-LT. W. C. M. CUBBAGE (Oxf. & Bucks. Lt. Infty.)
  SEC.-LT. H. F. HORNE (Oxf. & Bucks. Lt. Infty.)
  SEC.-LT. E. A. F. KEEN
  SEC.-LT. E. H. SOUTHAM
  SEC.-LT. A. G. STEWART

CAPT. A. F. L. SHIELDS (R.A.M.C.)
* SEC.-LT. T. D. BENNETT
SEC.-LT. W. A. MARTIN
SEC.-LT. E. HOBSON
SEC.-LT. C. H. WELTI
* SEC.-LT. H. D. O. PRESTON
SEC.-LT. E. G. BLACKMORE
SEC.-LT. C. BLICK
* SEC.-LT. A. R. PRICE
SEC.-LT. W. D. FRANCIS
LT. H. C. E. MASON
CAPT. THE REV. W. J. BELL (C.F.)
CAPT. THE REV. C. C. HAMILTON (C.F.)

A List of the Officers who served with the Battalion whilst it was still in England and their rank at the time of such service

---

MAJOR J. H. HOOKER, T.D.
MAJOR J. CHADWICK, T.D.
SURG.-CAPT. J. C. BAKER
CAPT. LORD ADDINGTON
CAPT. A. P. LIST
CAPT. G. H. SIMPSON
LT. R. A. BUCKMASTER
† MAJOR R. W. HARLING (Brigade Major)
† CAPT. S. R. VERNON (Brigade Staff Capt.)
CAPT. G. T. HANKIN
LT. THE HON. W. FREMANTLE
LT. R. T. HUGHES
SEC.-LT. J. E. FIRMINGER
SEC.-LT. R. C. NORWOOD
SEC.-LT. R. E. M. YOUNG
SEC.-LT. J. B. HALES
SEC.-LT. S. D. BISHOP
SEC.-LT. G. A. WYLLIE
SEC.-LT. O. FORDHAM
SEC.-LT. H. J. PULLMAN
LT. B. GREEN
SEC.-LT. N. B. WILLIAMSON
CAPT. L. L. C. REYNOLDS
SEC.-LT. J. C. SANFORD
SEC.-LT. W. R. HEATH
SEC.-LT. F. G. VAUGHAN
SEC.-LT. E. G. H. BATES
SEC.-LT. H. J. PRATT
SEC.-LT. F. H. ROVER
SEC.-LT. B. C. RIGDEN
SEC.-LT. W. H. HOFF
SEC.-LT. J. D. D. RENFREW (Scottish Rifles)
SEC.-LT. T. ROGERS (The Royal Scots)
SEC.-LT. V. F. GOULD (E. Yorks. R.)

*Denotes that the Officer was Wounded whilst Serving with the Battalion

†Denotes that the Officer Crossed to France with the Battalion in May, 1916

Where an Officer was Attached from Another Unit his own Regiment is shown in Brackets

Many of the Other Officers, whose names appear in this Record, went "Overseas," were Killed, Wounded, and Gained Distinctions. These facts are only shown Herein if they happened whilst the Officer in question was Serving with the 2nd Bucks Battalion

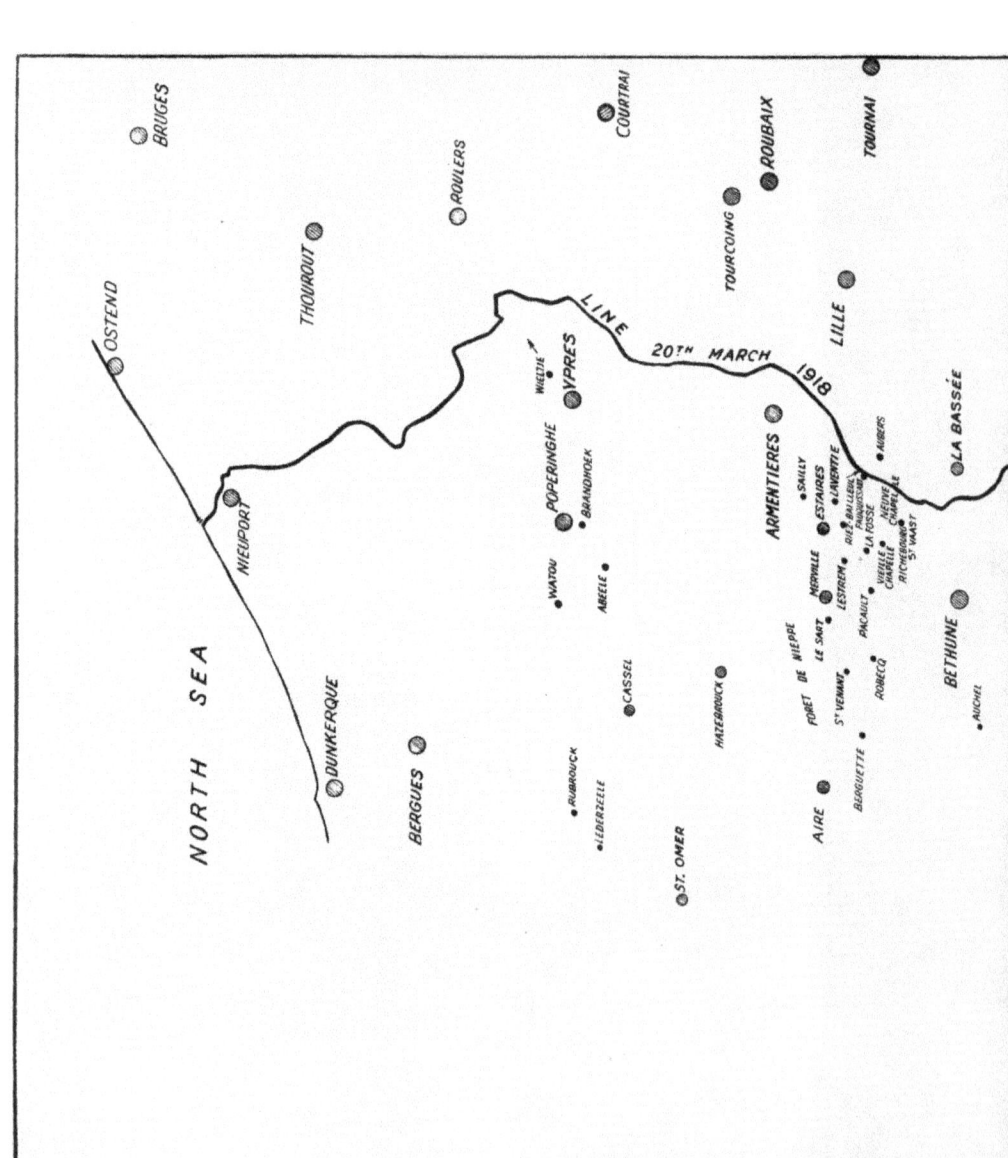

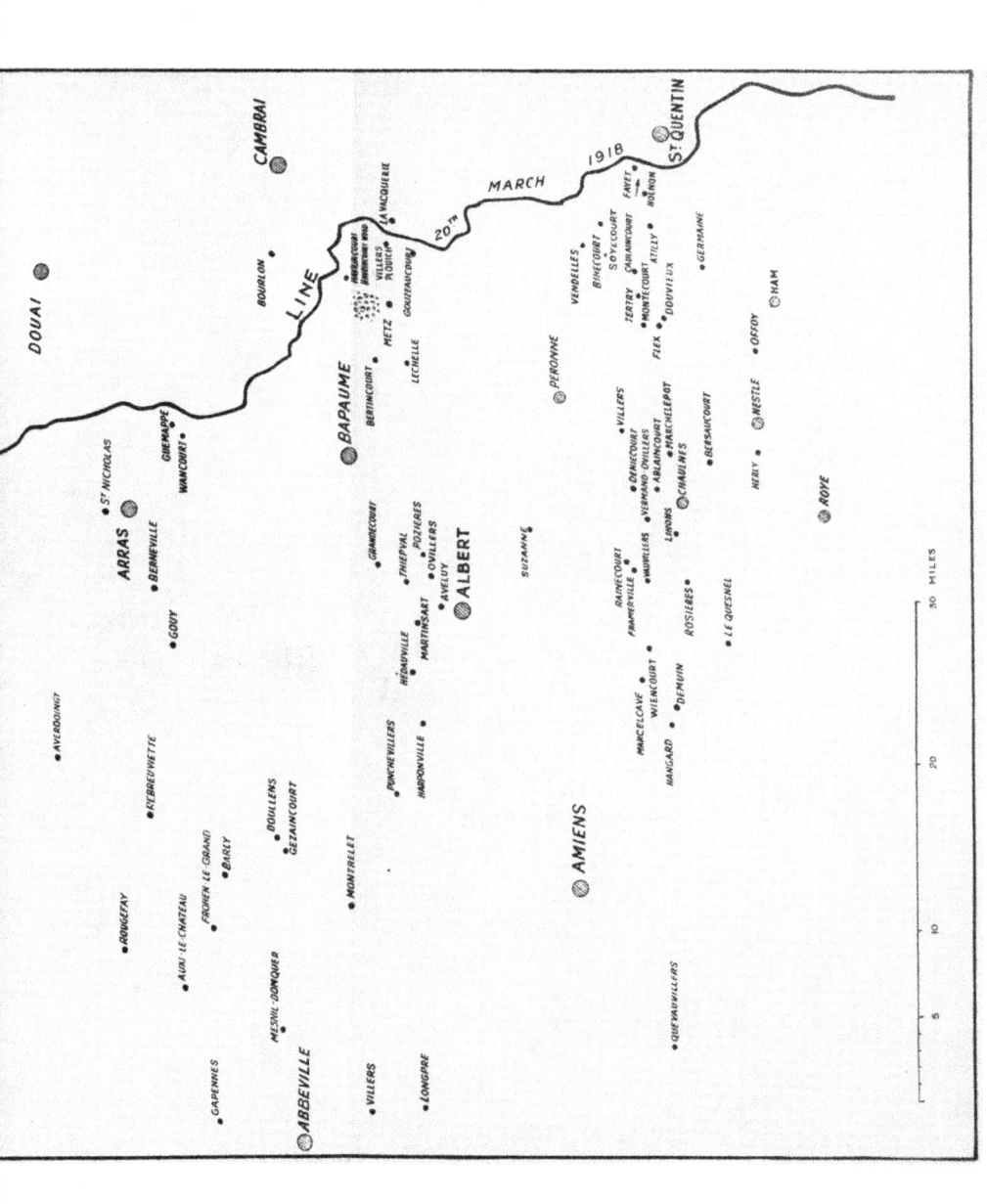

www.ingramcontent.com/pod-product-compliance
Lightning Source LLC
Chambersburg PA
CBHW071013160426
43193CB00012B/2037